My Zaida
A Collection of Literary Works

My Zaida

A Collection of Literary Works by
the Late Eleanor Horowitz Cullick

Suzanne Hetherington

XULON PRESS

Xulon Press
2301 Lucien Way #415
Maitland, FL 32751
407.339.4217
www.xulonpress.com

© 2019 by Suzanne Hetherington

All rights reserved solely by the author. The author guarantees all contents are original and do not infringe upon the legal rights of any other person or work. No part of this book may be reproduced in any form without the permission of the author. The views expressed in this book are not necessarily those of the publisher.

Printed in the United States of America

ISBN-13: 978-1-54566-306-6

A collection of the literary works by the late Eleanor Horowitz Cullick…

A descendant of the Davidic lineages of Shapiro and Horowitz…

A daughter of Abraham, Isaac, and Jacob by birth

And a child of Adonai by faith in Yeshua HamaShiach!

Compiled and provided by Suzanne Hetherington

TABLE OF CONTENTS

INTRODUCTION..ix

MY ZAIDA – A MEMOIR...1

SHAKESPEARE and HEDDA in the BRONX 9

THE RED COAT – A MEMOIR 15

REAL LIFE MIRACLES — 8-13-1960 17

REFLECTIONS 21

THE SACRIFICE–A TRUE STORY 27

EPILOGUE 29

INTRODUCTION

It was Shabbat, and we were having oneg before our afternoon Torah study at Beth Yeshuah HaMaschiach Messianic Jewish Congregation in Houston, Texas.

I was rapidly ushered through a myriad of dining table and chairs to where Ms. Eleanor was seated. She was a picture of elegance and refinement. Sylvia, one of the teachers at this congregation immediately began the intricacies of introducing me to Ms. Eleanor. .who was often affectionately called Ms. Ellie by those people who came to love her.

She was charming, and full of graciousness, with a hint of mischievousness about her. After conversing a while, we soon discovered that our life experiences were intricately interwoven via common people and places we had known or been. All too soon, Torah study began and it was very interesting and included passionate teaching, visuals, and the provoking invitation to learn more about the Words of Adonai.

When it was over, Eleanor was open to receive me as a new friend and I was invited to go with her and Sylvia to see her little "hovel" in the downtown neighborhood in Houston.

This was the first day, of many days that I was to be a frequent guest and helper to Ms. Ellie during the last two years of her life.

One of the goals we had planned together was the publishing of her works. It had been her desire to have completed it before she graduated to Heaven but it was not possible at that time due to her declining health and abilities.

And so it is that now I am publishing it for her and with the blessings of the late Rabbi Jim Pratt – who had had legal care of her until she passed on. I am thankful to them to be able to carry out one of her last desires.

Another goal we had had was to locate some of Ms. Ellie's relatives; and help her learn more about her genealogy. She was the granddaughter of survivors of the Holocaust–Horowitz and Shapiro lineages, both of whom were from Vilna, Poland. Her Grandfather (Zaida) had expressed that her family was distantly related to the Great Rabbi Vilna Gaon – of Vilna, Poland. Some of her other relatives came from Lithuania; but they all ended up in the Bronx in New York City.

It is from the neighborhood of Pelham Parkway in the Bronx, where Eleanor grew up and absorbed the nuances of this evolving Jewish-American area. She often referred to herself as a JAP – Jewish American Princess.

In this book, MY ZAIDA, Eleanor colorfully expresses the scenes of her childhood. She tenderly shares of her love for her Zaida – her grandfather.

It is my sincere hope that you enjoy and gain insight into the heart of this Jewish woman; who so passionately sought to live out her life for so many causes – and who was sought after and found by her Beloved Jewish Messiah, Yeshua Hamashiach – as He seeks after ALL His Lost Sheep –

Suzanne Hetherington

MY ZAIDA – A MEMOIR

My Zaida (grandfather) drank his hot tea from a clear glass; a sugar cube in his mouth. The golden liquid sipped or "zupped" – a delicate slurping sound followed by a sigh that bespoke of his intense satisfaction with the brew – an exhale of breath, a mechiah (pleasure). He would pick up the cloth napkin and dab at his lips and the edge of his white beard and mustache.

Zaida always had a beard. A pious Jew from Vilna in Poland, the home of the Vilna Gaon (of Blessed Memory), a holy man, the wisest of wise men, he was rumored to be a distant cousin.

Pelham Parkway, the Bronx, neighborhood of Jews, first generation like me, crowding the public schools, hardly any goyim (non-Jews). On the High Holy Days, there were no more than two dozen children in the entire school – (many students stayed out even though they were not Jewish) – and classes were not really held. Now, I don't know this for a fact, because I wasn't there for Heaven's sakes! I only know that when I returned after the holiday, we picked up where we had left off in our textbooks; and classes went back to normal.

I don't know why I wasn't in shul during those years. It was only when I reached my twenties that I began to attend the large, modern synagogues and temples, where services were held in Hebrew and English- and I was able to make some kind of connection. The shul was in a small building. It almost was an extension of our apartment house on Holland Ave. I never ventured inside, although the sight never failed to fill me with awe when the door was opened. I'd sometimes go and take a peek–and there were men, old men in tallits (prayer shawls) and wearing yarmulkes (skullcaps). A dim room with a golden light was on. Everything in dark tones as men in black suits davened (prayed), swaying back and forth in some type of religious ecstasy. Their sounds of rapture frightened the seven year old me. I could never find my Zaida, but he must have been there. For he left the apartment he shared with Grandma and Devora, my maiden aunt, early in the morning; and didn't return until early evening.

The burden of being known as the "maiden aunt" came years later for Devora. But I do believe the word "maiden" was used not only to signify Devora's singlehood or non-marital status; but also, her virginity as well. We didn't talk about that, of course. There must have been young men in Devora's life at one time; but if she dated, I never knew about it.

Devora's closest friend was a wild redhead, Irene, a "fast" girl with a head of bright curls framing a divine face, blue eyes, bright red lips, milky skin, and a zaftig figure to match a happy, carefree personality. Irene played the piano, sang, and danced. Wherever she went, fun was her companion. I adored her! I think she was a frustrated musical comedy "wannabe"; and when she eventually married- in her mid-forties, it was to a dull, electrician some years her junior. He was said to make a good living because he was able to buy his way into the union. He had dark, pomaded hair and a pencil-thin mustache. Irene would have Devora and me over for coffee and cake; attired in bright colors, in her high heels. She would flash some leg as she danced coquettishly through one of the current Broadway hits. Her husband smiling at this irrepressible creature he had had the good fortune to call his wife.

On Pelham Parkway, I lived in a large apartment on the third floor with my parents, my older brother Norman, my mother's widowed sister Reba, and Reba's daughter Clara – who was only three months younger than Norman. Zaida's apartment was on the floor above at a left angle to ours; so that we could call upstairs through the window to talk. No one we knew had a phone at that time, but the "yoo-hoos" via the window rivaled any electronic communication of today. And somehow, I don't know quite how, if you had to speak to another relative a few blocks away, the message got through. All news travelled fast.

When I climbed the stairs one flight to see Zaida, the aromas of Grandma's endless cooking and baking permeated the hallway. On Friday, the Sabbath chicken would be simmering in a large pot, broth delicately topped with glubules of fat, so rich was the stock and "light-as-air" kneidlach (dumplings) swam. A slice of carrot would seductively peek through the kneidlach which were made of matzo meal, eggs, and rendered chicken fat. Grandma made her own Challah, the braided bread, still warm from the oven. When Zaida returned from shul, we would gather around the cloth covered table. Their best china and silver was laid out, a carafe of red wine providing the only splash of color. The candles would be lighted by Grandma. Her head covered with a square black cloth, the flickering flames momentarily softening the angular planes of her face, as she prayed the Kaddish.

It wasn't until many years later that her personality underwent a radical change. She was never an easy woman, but old age brought a harshness in her countenance; that only now do I recognize as senility;that speedily overtook her after Zaida died. She eventually became incontinent and had to be put into a nursing home...when Devora, the daughter who had sacrificed her life to take care of her parents could no longer cope. (I was in college by then.) When Grandma died, I do not recall feeling any sadness; for the woman I knew as a child had ceased to exist years before; and the cronie she had become was no one I knew.

Zaida, however, was a sweet man, a man of infinitesimal patience and goodness. I never heard him speak a harsh word nor complain. He dressed in a black suit every day of his life; a suit with a vest, an immaculate white shirt and a dark tie. Completing the sartorial splendor of this ensemble, a black fedora on his head, the rolled brim turned up. There was never any variation. .summer and winter…he was the same. The only concession made to the harshness of the northern winter was a button-down sweater under his vest and a heavy black overcoat covering it all.

He had been a fine tailor in Poland! But the years of toiling by candlelight had taken its toll; and he could no longer see how to do the fine stitching. He wore thick-lensed glass…the magnified eyes now a milky blue. He still read the Daily Forward, a progressive Yiddish language newspaper – as did most of his generation in New York. And although I attended an Arbeiter Ring (Workman's Circle) school after my last class at P.S.105 – to learn how to read and write their beloved Yiddish; I never could master its intricacies. My teacher, Mr. Mendelson, tall, dark, intellectual, of a kind nature, would sit with me speaking beautifully modulated Yiddish, his English precise, almost theatrical – only slightly accented. I thought him to be very handsome!

Zaida knew no English. When he brought his wife and four daughters to this country; only the eldest daughter, Reba, was married. Zaida worked side-by-side with his son in law. By the time the two remaining daughters were married and with families of their own; Zaida had turned the business over to Reba's husband, who expanded, gained a modest reputation, and did exceptionally well.

In our home, only English was spoken to us- Norman, me and the children- except when my parents didn't want us to understand what they were saying. Eventually I understood; but by some tacit agreement – never let on that I did. A Jewish neighborhood, an enclave never to be encroached upon by outsiders, even to this day. We were within walking distance to the Bronx zoo – where I spent many wondrous hours. And was, many years later, to take my own "southern-born" children – and to watch them step back into my history. I have pictures of them atop of a camel – although I have no memory of seeing a camel as a little girl – so I assume this attraction was added for the more sophisticated of my childrens' generation.

There is a sweetness, a kindness, a sense of communal love in these sepia-toned mind pictures: Zaida, my Grandpa, always in the shul – a kindly, be-whiskered gentleman, to my child's eyes – old- even then. His English non-existent, so I either sank or swam; and I preferred to swim. And I would sit upon his lap as he told me stories in Yiddish of his own youth in Poland. Grandpa belonged as did the entire family to a fraternal organization of immigrants from the old country – traveling God knows where, all over the city with directions written on a small piece of paper – welcoming the newly-arrived greeners, the new ones, educating them in the ways of this new land where money, if you worked hard, was yours to earn and keep. The sounds of the horses' hooves of the Cossacks eventually becoming faint in Zaida's mind were replaced by the modern sounds of the Bronx.

It must have been apparent to poor Devora, after both her sisters married, that someone had to take care of their aging parents – and her fate was sealed. Devora, the Devoted. Her thoughts, lost dreams, desires (Did she have any she would even dare give voice to?) were kept to herself; and she spent the rest of her life as Aunt Devora to her nieces, nephews, and grand-nieces, and grand-nephews…even to the third generation. She died as had her mother – alone in a nursing home – the last of her family.

I called her once a month to get the family news to her until she could no longer care for herself; and gave up the apartment where she had lived for over forty years. The dreadful last winter of her life, I went to New York to see her, taking one of my daughters with me. Trudging in foot-high snow, I found her, scarcely recognizeable, sitting alone by a window and staring out at nothing. She did not know me at first, but when I said my name, she lifted her hand to touch my face…Is this the fate of the women in my family??? I wondered…Grandma, Mama, and now Devora…and where will I fit into this scheme of life and death???

When I was eleven, all of us left Pelham Parkway and moved into a large house. Mama, Daddy, Norman my brother, Aunt Reba and Clara, her daughter, Grandma and Zaida and Aunt Devora all nine of us living together. These things combined to make those years the most gentlest of my life: the sights and sounds, the aromas of hot pastrami and corned beef in the delicateson , sturgeon, whitefish, and pickles at the dairyman, all gone with my childhood! I was excited by the move, not realizing then, that a moment in time would forever be left behind- irretrievable, except in my memory.

The sweetness of that time, its innocence, can now be found in sepia-toned photographs. I have a "memory table" on which I have displayed my family in the privacy of my study. I look at them and touch briefly on my childhood. How young Mama and Daddy look in their wedding picture. And there's Uncle Joe's new car with the rumbleseat (he had courted Aunt Reba for years and they had eventually married). And here's a photo of Devora. She looks beautiful – one could weep for her lost life – for the husband she never held, and the children she never bore!

This was the first time Zaida, Grandma, and Devora lived under the same roof with all of us. I guess it must have taken some adjusting; but I was was young, happy, and somehow we managed.

In Europe, unrest and concern brought many more Eastern Jews to this country. Sadly, an uncle I never met, Zaida's oldest child and only son, had come to these shores with his parents and sisters – worked for a year in anticipation of sending for his own wife and two young children. But one day he simply returned to Poland. I was never told why; but when I asked Mama once, she said he just didn't like it here. So he went back to Vilna. By the time Jews were desperate to get out of there anyway they could – it was too late! He, his wife, and young daughter died in the ovens in Auschwitz.

The only remaining survivor of the death camp was a son named Phillip. He immigrated to Haifa, where he taught school for many years. After he retired, Phillip came with his wife to the states for a visit. When we met, my cousin Phillip looked at me, turned pale and wept. His strong arms encircled me, he kissed me, and I felt his tears on my cheek. Taking my face in his hands, speaking in Yiddish, I understood him to say that I looked like his sister who had died at Auschwitz.

Zaida would wait for me in the kitchen every day when I came home from elementary school. He would pour milk into a glass for me and place several of Grandma's cookies on a plate. We sat in silence as he zupped his tea. There was a shul on the next street. Our house was on a hill, its rear windows looking down to the shul. It was here on Saturday mornings, I could hear the sounds of the men at prayer. I think Zaida must have been the first of the men there for no matter how early I awoke, he would be gone.

So, now, I arrive at the point of a confession. It has been there, lurking in my memory, ready to leap out and confront me.

Zaida and Grandma kept a kosher home. No ifs, ands or buts!

Grandma cooked separately from us, using her own pots, and while Mama continued to buy meat and poultry from the kosher butcher; we did not strictly observe the separation of meat from dairy.

At Passover, the dishes were changed, but little by little, various exotic foods would somehow find their way into our icebox. After all, Norman and Clara, who were six years older than me, were American to the core; and although dating was limited to Jewish eligibility only; my brother at seventeen was obviously lusting after forbidden fruit. It was a short leap to forbidden foods.

I was the culprit who brought the treif (non-kosher) foods into the house – BUT they urged me on – and in a lifelong effort to please, I could never say no. I bought pork – bacon! There…it's out! The three of us discovered a mutual taste for this strange, but delicious meat; and I was the designated cook. It even tasted sinful! To the best of my recollection, Clara had never put her hands in or on anything that faintly resembled work! However, I enjoyed cooking and baking – especially my brother's favorite – chocolate cake! Most of the time, he studiously ignored me, which from his teenage vantage point was quite understandable. When he was eighteen, and had a little car, Mama would talk him into taking me to the movies. I would become so nervous, my fingers forgot how to manage buttons and straps; and I would be petrified lest he leave without me. Well, what boy in his right mind looking for a little adolescent action would want to be saddled with a twelve year old sister?

Norman would sit in the car, impatient, the motor running; and I would fly out in a state of nerves, already out of breath. The trip to the movie house would be made in silence, but I didn't care, because he was undeniably the handsomest boy in the neighborhood; and the girls in their saddle shoes and bobby sox thought they might have an edge if they cozied up to me – the kid sister! Even though I was a nerd, although the word had not yet come into usage, I was too smart for them, me with my head in a book…pretending I didn't know what they were up to.

Watching my brother play basketball, his curly blonde hair, sturdy boy (yeah, he had sex appeal but I didn't know then that's what it was) and a smile that could melt stone. I'd see the movements of the fan club, swishing, batting their eyes, and smiling their dimpled smiles.

Back in the kitchen, I reigned ; the unmistakeable aroma of bacon in the air! We devoured our breakfast of bacon and eggs, bagels or pumpernickel with cream cheese and Zaida would come in sniffing the air. He never looked at the package – and I'm not sure he could have read the label anyway (unless it displayed a picture of a pig). Clara and Norman would keep their heads lowered over their plates as I was busy doing the clean -up job. "Vas ist dos?" Zaida might ask, and I'd murmur "beef" – my face flushing. Surely he could smell my guilt, if not the bacon. But he never said a world. In his slippers, Zaida shuffled back to the parlor.

Yes, that's the burden of guilt I have carried for half a century! I would like to think that God forgives the child of long ago, who now, in her dotage, pays homage to one who deserved better!

Zaida was a one-man welcoming committee for the new arrivals in America. Without a word of English, nor the ability to read it, he ventured out into the teeming metropolis of New York City; and sometimes to that foreign country called Brooklyn, a slip of paper in his pocket with directions and all the information he needed to board buses and trains, and traverse the subterranean depths, to walk strange streets and arrive at his destination. To my knowledge, he never got lost! From the Bronx to Coney Island is no small feat, but Zaida did it! Well into his eighties, the sights and sounds of war, planes, rumbling tanks and troops wearing the dreaded swastikas, seeing his two grandsons go off to fight for their country – he continued on his rounds.

He might be on the dock as the ship came into the harbor. Other times he might be in the offices of the sponsoring agency. Sometimes Zaida was seen getting the freshly-scrubbed apartment ready for new tenants; women wearing babushkas, holding the hands of their frightened children after an arduous journey. The husbands were uneasy with the burden of providing for their families in this new land. All encountered the sight of my Zaida welcoming them to their new country!

He would bend down and with quivering hands stroke the heads and pat the cheeks of the children. The "greeners" had arrived, and my Zaida was there! In all kinds of weather, no one ever took a charge with more devotion than he – in the hundreds of journeys he made to meet his land's men.

One night after eating an early dinner, my Zaida lay down to rest and as unobtrusively and peacefully as he went through his life, he left it!

The old men from the shul all came to his funeral the next day, those from Perham Parkway, as well as from our new neighborhood. And the "greeners" showed up in gratitude to honor the old Jew who was there to greet them in their time of confusion and anxiety.

I saw him depart on these journeys and I saw him return, tired but happy. I would watch him pour water from the tap into the tea kettle, strike a match, and light the gas range. Measure the tea leaves into his glass, and pour in the boiling water – a spoon resting in the glass so that it would not crack – and then, sit down, take a sugar cube into his mouth and when the tea was ready, lift the glass and take a zup.

I see him sitting there in his black suit and yarmulke and hear him as he places the glass in its saucer. Lean back and sigh with satisfaction! Such a mechiah!

SHAKESPEARE and HEDDA in the BRONX

I was five years old when I saw my first Broadway play. It wasn't exactly on Broadway, but it was the beginning of my life-long love affair and eventual involvement with the strange and wonderful world of the THEATER!

The Fordham Theater was a legitimate house where almost new, and not-so-new plays with first-rate casts could be seen for as little as fifty cents a ticket.

These productions were presented in the Bronx; and, I assume, the other boroughs as well–what Manhattanites had available in abundance!

We had what came to be known as the Subway Circuit. From Pelham Parkway, where I lived, it was a twenty minute- five cents per bus ride to Fordham Road, which ran for several miles, and past an area which came to be known as Little Italy. Flanked on one side by the Bronx Zoo and on the other side by Fordham University, and converged into the Grand Concourse. This Grand Concourse was a lovely tree-laden boulevard, an esplanade running down its center, studded with apartment buildings predominantly populated by upper-scale Jews.

Nationally known, as well as privately owned fine shops dotted the Grand Concourse; but at its apex with Fordham Road stood Alexander's, the largest department store in the Bronx! The Concourse terminated at one end at 161st Street with Yankee Stadium and the Bronx County Courthouse which still stands, the Lady Liberty holding the scales of Justice in her hand.

On the other side of Fordham Road, at Alexander's, one continued on the Concourse to a graceful, but ample neighborhood park. It was in this park, that a band appeared for summer concerts in the large gazebo. The park boasted a tiny cottage once inhabited by the poet, Edgar Allen Poe. Its ceilings so low that someone only five feet ten would have to stoop.

My Aunt Reba started taking me to Saturday matinees and I don't know if my Cousin Clara, her daughter who was six years older than me, just didn't care to go or was busy with her own friends, or whether Aunt Reba loved theater so much that she would rather take a small child with her than to attend alone. Whatever the reason, what started out to be a one-time outing, because she had wanted my company, proved to be so successful, that soon; these occasional Saturday matinees on the Subway Circuit, a seasonal enterprise, expanded into forays to Manhattan as well, to the REAL thing, in the area of Broadway and 42nd Street!

And, in case you're wondering, my first experience was NOT a children's production, but a play named BROOKLYN U.S.A. – a story about ice, murder, cops and bad guys. It starred Elliott Nugent.

It was a warm, sunny day, bright, the bustle of Fordham Road and its shops adding to my contained excitement! My Aunt Reba window shopped, and we talked about the dresses, purses, shoes, and other apparel. I added my comments about the merit of a particular piece being already a critic of fashion at my tender age of five.

I was so happy that someone in my family was taking me somewhere that it would never have occurred to me to be a nuisance! Indeed, a much older cousin of dating age, urged on, perhaps by her mother, would take me with her when she went walking in the park with her would-be swains. It may be hard to understand a five year old as a designated chaperone, but I imagine lugging me around would be discouraging to any young man intent on getting fresh. Thus, when my cousin was taken for a malted; a tall glass of the delicious fountain concoction would be placed before me; as well as, in front of my cousin. Life could NOT have been better!

Many years later, Aunt Reba commented on how wonderful it was to take me places because I always behaved – not a bad recommendation!

In fact, I never became blasé about theater! After some years, I went on stage myself – well, that's another story!

Back to the Fordham Theater, stepping from the brightness of the day and into that cool, darkness of the theater; portraits of handsome men and beautiful women majestic in costume gracing the foyer; watching my aunt purchase our tickets at the box office. Holding her hand as we began to climb the carpeted staircase leading up to the mezzanine – I was enthralled!

Our seats were in the first row. And as I leaned over the rail and looked down, I counted the rows of seats below. It was like sitting in the front row before an orchestra – but better. because I didn't have to bob my head to see over the person in front of me. The curtain covering the stage was red velvet and looked so luxurious to my childish eyes. I didn't see it was already faded and worn. For this curtain represented glamour – from the lobby with the box office inside to the vivid velvet of the seats. You see, I hadn't yet realized this was NOT a movie house!

Aunt Reba handed me the slender program which she knew I could read. I whispered questions to her which she patiently answered. We were among the first arrivals, but soon the theater started to fill up. I could tell this was different because everyone spoke in low voices. Also, I didn't see any other young people there. When Clara took me to the movies on a Saturday, it would be mobbed with neighborhood kids and sometimes we'd all sit through the feature twice!

The lights dimmed. There was an expectant murmur, some movement. Then, as the curtain drifted up into the ceiling, I gasped–It's real! I said to myself! I don't remember breathing for the next two hours except in one scene. I had already learned that when the curtain came down for a few minutes, these were called scenes.

My memories of that production filter through the clouds of time. While I can see the set: realistic, gritty, this is only one scene that made an indelible impression on me. A blonde woman actually undressed. She took off her skirt, lay down on a bed. Mr. Nugent removed his jacket and loosened his tie and joined her! I couldn't believe it! They were going to sleep right there in front of everyone!

Now you have to understand that at the age of five, I didn't comprehend the significance of this. I didn't remain innocent for very long. By the time I saw my first play in London, an enigma by Harold Pinter – and the couple joined each other in bed au buffe – I knew!

If my Aunt Reba had any misgivings about having exposed me at such a tender age to carnal sin, she never said a word. But, since it didn't corrupt me, it proved to be the measure by which I gauged my own children's stage and film experiences – which were fairly sophisticated at an early age.

Afterward, Aunt Reba took me to a restaurant for Chinese – my very favorite food in the whole world!

The Goldbergs, Molly and Jake, a warm and funny slice of Jewish life as I knew it- with Molly's "yoo-hoos Mrs. Bloom !" out the window to her neighbor was as familiar to me as an old shoe. And why not? That neighborhood was mine!

"Abie's Irish Rose" taught tolerance for intermarriage through comedy. "Golden Boy" where I heard the incredibly sweet sounds of a violin for the first time- really heard it because that instrument was such an integral part of the play. Jane Cowl as "Hedda Gabler" a tall, magnificent woman, dressed all in black. Those last moments when I knew something awful was going to happen, and I didn't dare blink my eyes – didn't dare breathe – one second, two seconds, three, four, five…a shot! I cried out as did some women in the audience (quietly, of course). And the curtain calls, the thrill of seeing my idol, now out of character, deeply bow or stand serenely, hands clasped in front, a nod of the head acknowledging the applause, the cries of "bravo!"

My child's voice ringing out loud and "oh my God! She looked up at me, Aunt Reba, she sees me – and the stage would waver through my tears!

Ethel and Lionel Barrymore, Paul Muni, and Eva LeGalliene, who raised her incandescent eyes that bored into mine – so beautiful then and so beautiful in her late seventies when I saw her the last time – still holding that stage, that audience, as no one ever did before or since!

Six wonderful, magical years of the Subway Circuit! I don't know whether the old Fordham Theater is still there. if only as a landmark.but probably not. I have thought of going back and retracing the steps taken a lifetime ago;but I guess not. Some things are best left to memory.

I saved some programs all through the years of my theater going; and eventually there were so many. I stored them in Playbill binders where, one day, many years and hundred of plays later, when I no longer lived at home; they were thoughtlessly thrown away.

When I was eleven, we moved; all of us to a large house; not really far but almost a world away from my childhood and Pelham Parkway. Close to New Rochelle, we were on the cusp of Westchester County. Reba would take me into the city to Manhattan, with all its theaters and restaurants. She took me to Radio City Music Hall where the Rockettes continue to dazzle, and in the winter, we would sit beside the ice rink at Rockefeller Center sipping hot chocolate and watching the skaters.

Everything eventually changes. My Cousin Clara got married. So did Aunt Reba. But by that time, I was going to my Saturday matinees with a friend or even alone. I became most discerning, and when the treasure of the fifties: Those years of "Death of a Salesman", "Born Yesterday", "the Glass Menagerie", "Peer Gynt", "Darkness at Noon", The Bad See" Lee J Cobb, Arthur Kennedy, Judy Holliday, Laurette Taylor, John Garfield, Fredric March, and Florence Eldridge in O'Neill's "Long Day's Journey into Night. Brando and "A Streetcar Named Desire" and the wealth of British imports: Olivier, Leigh, Redgrave. I knew theater as few children did. I became charged with good taste, a keen eye, and a great appreciation for those who gave and continue to give a visceral excitement as no other medium can.

Eventually, I studied with Uta Hagena and Herbert Berghof and built my own small resume; but life does have a way of coming full circle!

My OWN children, not too many years older than me when I saw my first play were taken to New York; and I purchased tickets for them to see:

"The Great White Hope" with James Earl Jones and Jane Alexander. It was this play which had a scene occurs where Ms. Alexander is in bed and Mr. Jones joins her – well…

This is where I came in…

THE RED COAT – A MEMOIR

*M*ama made all of my clothes. It wasn't until I was in my early teens that I had my first store-bought dress. The experience of going with Mama into the dress shop – where she fingered the material and inspected the seams challenged anyone's patience! Mama's experienced fingers and knowing eyes finding unseen faults to anyone else's work.

This scenario was accompanied by my desire to crawl into any hole I could find. All I had wanted was the dress!

I didn't care that the stitches weren't perfect. Mama saw things that no normal eye could. And the longer this process took, I felt the dress was beginning to slip away from me. By some miracle, eventually, we brought it home. This was where Mama swiftly and efficiently worked her magic by smoothing out puckered seams and eliminating whatever seamstress sins she might have found. Her foot pedal sewing machine humming as she bent over the fine fabric. Finally, with one swoop, the transformation of a shmata (a rag of a dress) into a work of art was completed!

I don't remember what happened to that dress – or to all the subsequent dresses that I've bought through the years. Where do old clothes go??

But, I do remember my red coat!

The streets of Pelham Parkway in the Bronx, my neighborhood for the first eleven years of my life are my sweetest memories!

Sounds of Yiddish were being spoken between friends, shopkeepers, Mama and her three sisters – but rarely between Mama and my Father.

In our large and airy one bedroom apartment; where did we all fit???

[Unfortunately, this is one of Eleanor's writings for which we found no ending to this memoir. During the years that I knew Eleanor, there was not a time that she did NOT have a red coat. So the red coat must have made an indelible impression upon her. I have since then learned that the wearing of a red coat is usually a reference to the suffering endured by the Jewish people during the pograms carried out during the Holocaust. One of the photos in this book shows Eleanor wearing her red coat to a memorial service to Holocaust Survivors and their descendants – of which she was one.]

This photo was when she had her very firstride in a truck to carry us to the service to honor Holocaust Survivors and descendants.Ms. Ellie was honored there as a descendant of her grandparents who had survived. This was the Spring before she passed on.

REAL LIFE MIRACLES — 8-13-1960

𝓘 sat down calmly on my sunroom sofa and looked outside at the lush, green, back lawn. The oak tree planted two years before when my husband and I moved into our newly-built home. The nursery was ready for its first occupant.

Earlier that morning, I had driven to our pharmacy, where I purchased the formula recommended by our pediatrician. He was a brilliant doctor, who handled the most unusual and difficult cases. I was in a position to know as I had worked for several years in the radiological department of the hospital. This hospital was built and staffed by the Sisters of Charity of the Incarnate Word. The obstetrician was also first rate. He called me this passed Thursday, August 11th at 6pm and told me that I was to be the mother of a baby girl – 7 lbs 6 oz. !

What was unusual was that I was also pregnant by only six months. With two previous miscarriages, and and an insatiable desire to be parents, it never occurred to either my husband nor myself to cancel this adoption – which had been secured through the services of an elderly attorney and this obstetrician.

As a Jewish couple, we had found it seemingly impossible to adopt a baby. We had faced the probability that obtaining a baby through agencies would be a dead-end – due to our Jewish religion. And so, we had contacted Abe Levinthal, a semi-retired attorney, who was dedicating his last years performing mitzvahs (good deeds) in placing babies in Jewish homes where religion was NOT a factor to the birth mother.

We were expecting our baby to be delivered to us at noon; when I was seen at the pharmacy stocking the cart with all manner of baby supplies. Word swept like wildfire through our small southern community. When I arrived at home, Nathan, my husband, happily told me the telephone had been ringing off the hook! I rushed to put the packages away! Then, I dashed into the nursery to check the spacious room filled with new French furniture, ivory, with one crib inscribed in gold "Sharon".

Also in the nursery, were a matching bureau drawers, a bathinette, and rocking chair which stood ready to welcome our baby. My mother who left our native New York to see her first grandchild was the picture of efficiency. The house shone! Recently delivered flowers were arranged throughout – awaiting our new arrival!

Our beloved baby girl, Sharon, arrived and was cradled in many arms of love! She hardly knew her crib for the desire of so many people to hold and shower her with love and affection. She had such a sunny disposition! But one day, I noticed our baby was cranky and refusing her bottle. She had a slight fever, so I called her pediatrician. He reassured me but after several hours, I noticed a change in the coloring of her skin – a blue tinge. I knew from my experience working in the hospital that she must not be getting enough oxygen. As our regular pediatrician was going out of town, He referred us to a Dr. Wedgeworth and so after relaying our situation to him; we immediately went to the meet him at the emergency room at the hospital!

We sped through the empty streets to the hospital. Upon arrival to the emergency room, Dr. Wedgeworth looked into Sharon's moth, delicately examining her jaw. He wasted no time and ordered surgery! Her oxygen intake had decreased and a tracheotomy had to be performed immediately!

Everything after that is a blur; except for one phone call to my best friend. Weeping, I told her what had happened. "I love this baby so, I cannot imagine loving the one I'm carrying with this all-encompassing love. I will die if Sharon dies".

Weakly I listened to the voice of reason on the other end of the line. Realizing that this was NOT about me, but about my baby girl Sharon; I also had to be strong for her and the baby I was carrying.

The nun with whom I had worked in radiology was Sister Mary Josephus. She led the way to the hospital room where I was to wait. She sat me down in a rocking chair and with her calm demeanor, asked me to pray with her. As in all Catholic hospitals, a cross was on the wall – and I reflectively raised my hand to touch the Star of David that I always wore around my neck. I listened to this wonderful nun's offer of prayer to a God we both shared.

When done, she knelt beside me and told me that she would bring my little baby to me as soon as she could. Sister Josephus gently touched my cheek and with the sweetest of smiles, left the room. I had stopped crying. I put the fate of my beautiful baby Sharon into God's hand, knowing that Nathan had called our Rabbi as well. Our synagogue was only two blocks away from the hospital.

I do not recall how long I waited. Eventually, the door opened and Sister Josephus wheeled an incubator into the room. She had a beautiful smile on her face. There my precious baby lay! The Sister gave thanks to God and quietly left us alone.

I looked at Sharon for a while. Then, placed my hand very carefully into the incubator and touched my baby daughter's tiny hand. I watched as her delicate hand opened up and held onto one of my fingers. A sweet smile appeared on her face as if she knew she was holding her mommy's hand. Nathan eventually appeared, his face lighting up with a smile as he drank in the beauty of his new child. During the remainder of the day, other Sisters of Charity came to visit this woman who had just "had a baby" and was six months pregnant!

Years later, long after Nathan and I were divorced, I relocated to Houston Texas. Sharon chose to remain in Shreveport, where she had been born and attend nursing school there. My other two children, also now grown, each one married and living in other states. Nathan was now an octogenarian and a widower – as his next wife had died some years later. It was in this setting, that I had had the pleasure of a visit from Sharon who came to see me in Houston. We had spent the afternoon shopping and sharing a lunch. The topic of her adoption and place in our family came up. She confessed feeling as if she didn't belong – that she and her siblings had become so different in all areas of living. I was stunned!

This beautiful young woman, my first born, had always wanted to become a registered nurse, and had succeeded in her choice of careers. She had given her father and me our only grandchild. Sharon now mentioned that she was aware how her Grandmother (my mother) had seemed to favor her over her siblings and she wanted to know why.

I explained, "because you were her first grandchild. She saw me in you – your coloring and smile. Yes, she loved the other grandchildren, but you were special – so beautiful! And until she died, you were her favorite (Alzheimer's did rob my Mama of precious memories in her latter years.) She would sit on the patio while you slept in your carriage, and never take her eyes off of you. She was afraid of someone stealing you." I had hoped in telling these little stories that they would put to rest any questions Sharon had regarding her adoption or of our love for her.

[Footnote: You will see in the next book ELEANOR...that at her most needy time, Sharon, the adopted daughter, was the only child to come to see her or help her.]

REFLECTIONS

Wilma had thought him to be quite ugly at first. She was even afraid of him. She felt pity; pity was logical.

Later, she would remember Norman's words rushing out in a rich, deep baritone – how she would listen! Norman sat quite still. His face was intense – even vibrant! His hands were long, the fingers supple – the hands of an artist.

He stared at her constantly. She could feel his presence. It required all her will that she could summon NOT to turn and face him.

The other people in the room were rising. She went with them into the small entrance hall. The door opened and they were gone. Her room now felt safe. Though she tried, thoughts of Norman became so real – almost physical. She said his name aloud – Norman. He had entered her life only two months ago being introduced to her as Carla's brother. His face had a "hospital" pallor. He was separated from his wife and out of the army – having returned back home to live with his family. Since his discharge, he had been someplace else a long time – his paleness was indicative of this.

It was ten and Wilma sat before the fireplace halfway dozing when the doorbell rang. She knew it would be Norman.

He sat with her before the fireplace and took the drink she offered. Norman acted like a man afraid to show that he wanted all of the drink at once. Suddenly, he went to the piano. He turned to Wilma and asked what she wanted to hear. She said, "Chopin". And then she felt stupid because everybody asks for Chopin!

As the music filled the room, she felt an almost hysterical giggle in her throat. The scene was from a B-movie – fireplace, glasses clinking, cigarette smoke and piano music.

Wilma began to relax. She looked at him and noticed he seemed quite vulnerable and lonely. This had not occurred to her –that Norman wanted to be her friend. Somehow Wilma knew that he would affect her life – yet, she brushed the thought aside.

During that next week, after Wilma got off work, Norman would meet Wilma at the train station. Then, they would walk together She did not know what Norman did during the day.

He did not paint. He said that he had been ill such that he could not get his mind back into it. Wilma went in for dinner and watched Norman return to his parent's house. Later in the evening, Wilma would look through the porch curtains and see Norman standing outside. He was looking at the house as if he could see through the brick walls.

When Wilma went out to him, she sensed her mother's disapproval because he was still a "married man". Sometimes she felt wicked. But then, when she would look up at Norman, who had never touched her; she didn't feel wicked at all.

They had been to a movie. Norman sat half-turned towards her, quietly looking at her until she felt tears coming into her eyes.

Later, outside the movie theater, Wilma breathed in the cool, night air and wanted desperately to be home, in her own room, in her own bed, away from this strange man of whom she knew nothing, of whom she pitied, and did not know why, and of whom she was afraid – and did not know why.

During the ride home in the taxi, they did not speak. Only when they were nearing their homes, did Norman mention his wife to whom he had been married just before his tour of duty in the army. They were young and in love. His wife had become pregnant too soon and remained at home with her mother while he was away in the army camp. He was overseas when she gave birth to their daughter. After that, Norman's wife's letters came less frequently. Then, they stopped! When he returned home from his service in the Army, he found that his wife's mother was caring for his little daughter; but his wife, Fay, had run off with another man a year ago. Wilma knew that there was much more than Norman had told her. His voice was monotone. His hands lay limp in his lap, and he said no more.

It was Saturday and Wilma was dressing to go out. Her mother came in as she was putting on her lipstick. "Are you going out with Norman again?" Wilma nodded yes, her lips pursed as she wielded the pink lipstick. "You should not see him so much! What if he should become sick…what would you do?" her mother continued.

This was what Wilma had known only dimly. The year unaccounted for before Norman had come to stay with his family. She wanted to know more, but not from her mother. So she replied, " it will be alright. He's been fine. Besides, I enjoy his company!"

Now why had she said that? Wilma did not really enjoy his company at all and her reply didn't satisfy her mother. Wilma quickly took the conversation to another channel – and so for a few moments they discussed Wilma's impending shopping trip- ending with a request for her to pick up some lotion.

Norman waited outside. They took the bus to 50th Street. Then, they casually walked to 5th Ave. Wilma found herself enjoying this little expedition. Norman had exquisite taste and seemed to take a very real interest in her purchases. He subtly supervised and she particularly happy and extravagant! It was noon! They window shopped up the avenue. Nothing escaped his eager eyes. He was absorbed in everything. The small import shops featuring the latest wear, the quaint antique shops, their ancient wares gleaming from windows which reflected the tall buildings. Norman loved every detail! He pointed out to her things that she would never have seen alone. She thought it must be in his artist's training that made him so wonderfully observant. Wilma was grateful for his skills. He seemed so happy!

They were hungry, so Norman suggested a cocktail and lunch. Wilma had thought this was terribly sophisticated. She had thought that people who drank before five were special. Wilma knew she was young and naïve.

They stepped off of the curb. A taxi bore down upon them fast with the horn blasting in the air! Norman had his hand firmly beneath her elbow and she felt a sharp pain.

Norman stood deathly still. His face was white in the autumn sun, his dark eyes panicky and confused. Norman suddenly left her, and bolted across the wide thoroughfare – ignoring the rush of oncoming traffic. People turned to look.

Wilma was stunned! She continued to cross the street. The thickening crowd of strangers caused her to lose sight of him. She rushed into the bodies of shoppers when – suddenly, she saw his tall frame. He was leaning up against a building, with his arms hugging himself tightly, and his head down. When Wilma reached him, she saw his closed eyes, tears streaming down his face, and was overwhelmed with compassion for this weeping young man.

Wilma put her arms around Norman and led him away down a side street. His body convulsed with sobs. A small lounge was the first place she saw and they entered it. After choosing a rear booth, which faced away from the door, Wilma sat with Norman. Whispering she knew not what, only trying to comfort him -trying to rid him of this nameless terror.

Slowly, Norman's sobbing subsided. Wilma knew he would be ashamed because of what it was that had taken hold of him out there and which she now had witnessed. She wanted to tell him that it was alright and that she understood. In actuality, she didn't, and so she said nothing.

Wilma must have ordered something because the waiter brought drinks to the table. Norman gripped his glass tightly, bringing it to his lips with both hands, which trembled. Wilma thought he was going to spill it. She watched him drink with his head down.

She wondered if he was an alcoholic, but she had not known any alcoholics or how they were supposed to act. Somehow, he just seemed sick, rather than an alcoholic.

At first, she thought he wanted another drink; but Norman asked to go home instead. She quickly put two dollars on the table, and they walked outside together. It was sunlight still and they hailed a cab and she took him home.

Wilma had forgotten the lotion for her mother in all of the commotion. She did not see Norman again for several weeks. She never entered her house without looking first toward his house, but he was never in sight. He had come quickly into her life and just as quickly was gone! Wilma thought that she might never see him again.

One day Norman was waiting for her at the station. The evening air was crisp and clear. She rushed over to him, but he didn't smile at her. And for the first time, Wilma thought he was ugly and wondered how she could have thought him as handsome. He told her that he wanted to paint her and that there was a friend's studio they could use. So she went with him. Afterwards, Wilma would look back on those days of her youth and think of them as most fulfilling. There were assuredly many happy times in the years ahead for her but never quite like this.

If they were happy for her, Norman seemed delirious with pleasure! He talked and painted. She loved to hear him and loved to watch him and have him watch her…she loved him!

With the painting almost finished, Wilma was afraid for them both. She knew he was in love with her and hoped he would not tell her.

The night the painting was done, she looked at it. Knowing little of talent nor of art, just feeling his love in the picture and feeling herself as beautiful. She took the champagne he offered and drank and laughed and loved.

If this was what it was all about, their meeting, all their times together- if this was the reason for it all, it would also be a partial reason for why it ended.

When Norman asked her to marry him, after painfully pointing out that he would have to get a divorce, that he had been ill and was still not well, that he was really being unfair to her; BUT that he loved and needed her so terribly and Never thought that he would be able to love or need a woman again —- Wilma saw the end of it. And she could do nothing to prevent it.

If only she were older, but she was not. There was so much that she did not know.

She tried to avoid him – hating herself for wanting them to love again and hating herself for avoiding him. Norman seemed to sense how she felt and made it easy for her. She loved him all the more for this; yet, hated herself all the more for this.

The shot that split the air that warm Indian summer night, the streets were still wet from the recent rain. That shot shocked Wilma into awaking from her restless sleep. She sat up in her bed and forced her mind to act. It was probably a car backfiring.

She went to the window and saw the auto. The driver was inspecting his rent tire. Seconds later, screaming started – terrible screaming! The sounds of havoc and Wilma knew it was Norman! She buried her head under the blanket trying not to hear and wept silently.

In the morning, groggy from her incomplete sleep, Wilma arose and stood before her window. She watched as the black limousine drove up before his house. She saw two men go inside. She felt her stomach turn and wanted to throw up. Then, the men came out.

Norman's mother was on one side of him and his father on the other. They supported his body which seemed so small. His tear stained face strained to look at the people watching him proceed to the car. His mother was crying.

Norman seemed to notice this for the first time and looked at her as a child would – in wonder as to what she might be crying about. When the men led him into the automobile, Wilma saw the terror on his face, she knew that he would be whimpering, "please, please".

His father entered the sedan, Norman and his mother following while the two men sat in the front and then they all drove off.

A tune whispered and danced around in Wilma's head:

When Johnny comes marching home again, Hurrah! Hurrah!

She hummed quietly to herself as she stood there, looking down at the quiet empty street.

The End

THE SACRIFICE–A TRUE STORY

As she backed the station wagon out of the driveway, Rosemary followed Joe who was behind the wheel of a rented U-Haul. She thought of the dozen more tasks awaiting her upon her return to the home they were leaving. It was Father's Day in 1973 and the Whitfield clan: Rosemary, Joe, and their nine children were moving.

It was almost twenty years since Rosemary and Joe had left New Orleans, where the young soldier's heart was captured by the lovely Creole girl. He had committed himself to her. Following his Army service, he returned to make her his wife.

Before they knew it, there were three children in three years; and Joe's salary wasn't enough to support his family. Prior to the Army, as an eighteen year old, Joe had worked for Neiman Marcus in Dallas. It was here that Stanley Marcus who partially owned Neiman Marcus store, was impressed by the handsome black youth. so reserved, polite, and industrious Joe had been. Thus, it was that when Joe realized he needed a better job,that he turned to the store owner, who, true to his word, had a job for him and welcomed back a good worker – Joe.

That first move to Dallas was hard for Rosemary. She would be leaving the city she loved and the comfort of a large, gregarious family. But there were holidays and reunion; and now, she would have room for her own brood as well as for her family.

Joe worked hard, and soon proved himself. His family continued to grow. His position with Neiman Marcus steadily improved. Now realizing their dream at last, the young couple were moving out of a crowded apartment and into a large, rambling house with ample space for their children. Remembering back to the day that she left her beloved South Louisiana, Rosemary wondered where the years had gone.

Returning now from her memories, Rosemary gave the two oldest children Debra aged 15 and John aged 14 the task of fairly assigning bedroom to the remaining children and for John to help his dad Joe with the heavy work. Ten year old Lydia was in the kitchen with Debra putting things in order and being assisted by Valerie aged nine. The responsibility of caring for the four younger children fell to 13 year old Glenn, who was Rosemary's sweet, gentle boy – a special joy among so many in her heart. It was Glenn who pointed out the perfect space in the backyard for Rosemary's longed-for vegetable garden. Glenn had a gift with the little ones. She knew she could count on him to see that they were fed. Such a good boy! He was fair-skinned like his mom and hard-working like his dad. And so it was that everyone was caught up in the excitement of their new home!

Glenn so rarely asked his mother for anything – preferring to earn his own money by doing chores for neighbors. He mowed lawns or washed windows for people he knew who needed this help. Only a few days before, he had asked Rosemary for a social security card so he could apply for a job on the newspaper to be a delivery boy.

They had neighbors who noticed this new family. The neighborhood had so many children ! One of the neighbors, Ginny Adams had a son named Billy, who went to an Episcopalian Church school. This was the first black family to move into this neighborhood. Ginny had felt at times that her children had been too isolated and needed to be friends with people from other races. So she told Billy that he could bring a casserole that she had prepared to this new family. She watched her precocious youngster walk down to the two story house – as a station wagon was backing out of its driveway. A tall boy seemed to have been left in charge of two little ones; and when Billy arrived, the older boy shook her child's hand. What a nice gesture she thought. These children have been well brought up. There were two little girls in the yard; and Billy and this older boy went over to them. It was a beautiful day. In thirty minutes, Ginny would check on her son Billy. You know, to make sure that all was going well. Ginny Adams Never saw her son alive again!

EPILOGUE

You have now experienced the colorful, dramatic flare from the pen of Ms. Eleanor Horowitz Cullick.

It is my hope that you have been able to see the passion she had for life. Yes, life was to be lived to the fullest and deeply experienced!

In Eleanor's life, the drama which she so loved on stage – studying under Uta Hagen and Herbert Berghof to actually acting at Centenary College 's Marjorie Lyons' Playhouse.

This drama actually became her reality – as two pivotal events in her life, greatly enhanced the downward slide: divorce and an event which cost her over a decade in prison. But, in the end, Ms. Ellie had victory by her receiving of Yeshua as her Mashiach.to save her soul. More of these things in the next book: ELEANOR, a Jewish princess meets her Jewish Messiah.

In all things, we give thanks to our Lord Jesus Christ for all His benefits – even to the God of our Salvation. Who loved us before we were born and loves us still, to draw us unto His salvation with cords of love – through people already in Him.

I want to thank the late Rabbi James Pratt , his wife Estella, Kathleen Elowitz, and Sylvia Van Bibber, Arlene Holton and Greg Edmonds for introducing me to Ms. Eleanor, and for their continued support during her last years of life.

A portion of book sales will be donated to Beth Yeshua Hamashiach Congregation and/or to orphans in the U.S. and Israel. Thank you for your interest and subsequent support of this ministry through your purchase.

Toda Rava!
Suzanne

PS As you can see on Eleanor's gravestone, she was a Jewish Believer in Yeshua – Hebrew name for Jesus.

www.ingramcontent.com/pod-product-compliance
Lightning Source LLC
LaVergne TN
LVHW081456060526
838201LV00051BA/1816